Everyday Cooking
Meat

Contents

Everyday Cooking

Cookbooks in this series:

Pasta

Meats

Poultry

Seafood

Vegetables

Entertaining

Soup & Salad

One-dish Meals

NICHOLS
Publishing Group
Imprint of Allied Publishing Group, Inc.
Copyright © 1999
Recipes by Jake Ratcliffe
Photos by Laszlo Studios
Printed in Canada

Beef-Rice Rolls

4 servings

1 cup white rice or a combination of
   white & wild rice, cooked
¼ cup mushrooms, chopped
¼ cup onions, chopped
1 pound lean round or flank steaks, cut
   to 4 inches square and pounded thin
Salt & pepper
Flour
2 tablespoons olive oil
2 cups stock, bouillon or dry wine
(1 teaspoon tomato paste)

1. Combine **rice**, **mushrooms**, and **onion**.

2. Divide the rice mixture among **steaks**; spread thinly to within ¼ inch of edges and season with **salt** and **pepper**. Form meat into rolls, securing each with string or toothpicks.

3. Dredge the meat rolls in **flour**, and brown them evenly in very hot **olive oil**.

4. Place rolls in an oven dish with **broth or wine**. Mix in **tomato paste** if desired.

5. Bake the rolls, covered, in a 300° oven for about 1 hour or until the meat is tender. Serve with gravy from the oven dish.

381 calories	455 mg sodium
23.2 gr fat	7.2 gr saturated

Beef Roll–Ups

Serves 4

1 pound lean round or flank steaks cut to
about 4 inches square
½ cup soft bread crumbs
2 eggs, hard-cooked and chopped
3 anchovy fillets, mashed
¼ teaspoon nutmeg, freshly grated
8 ounces cooked spinach, chopped
2 cups chicken broth

1. Place **beef** between sheets of wax paper or
   clear food wrap and gently pound to
   about ¼-inch thickness.
2. Combine **bread crumbs, eggs, anchovies,**
   and **nutmeg** with **spinach.** Divide the
   stuffing, arrange in strips across each of
   the meat squares and roll them up. Secure
   rolls with toothpicks or string.
3. Place rolls in a well-greased oven dish
   with **broth.** Bake for 1 hour at 300˚, or
   until beef is tender.
4. Remove beef to a serving platter and keep
   warm. Reserve pan juice for making gravy.

316 calories	558 mg sodium
18.8 gr fat	7.1 gr saturated

Beef Roll–ups **may be made with fresh or
frozen spinach.** Fresh spinach should be
rinsed well by tossing in water to release
sediment, then cooked briefly, covered, in
only the moisture that clings to the leaves.
Frozen spinach need only be defrosted.

Chicken broth is recommended for the
liquid, but vegetable broth will do as well. A
hearty beef broth or red wine will produce a
darker gravy.

Anchovies are not essential to this dish,
but they reinforce flavors without adding a
"fishy" taste.

**Fresh nutmeg is vastly superior to
ground.** Stored in the freezer, the seeds will
retain their freshness for years.

Corned Beef & Cabbage

2 pound corned beef brisket
1 head cabbage, about 2 pounds, cored

1. Rinse and wipe the **beef** to remove any residual brine from the surface. Place in a pot with sufficient water to completely cover. Bring to a boil slowly and cover. Simmer gently for 2 hours or until the meat is easily pierced with a fork. Skim off any froth that forms on the surface of the water.

2. Cut the **cabbage** head into wedges and place in the pot with the beef for the final 15 minutes of cooking or until cabbage is tender.

   Note: If the pot is not large enough to hold the cabbage with the beef, remove the beef when it is done and cook the cabbage in the liquid.

3. Allow beef to stand for 10 or 15 minutes before carving, then cut into thin slices across the grain.

4. Serve the cabbage wedges topped with thin slices of corned beef.

5. Provide plenty of fresh or prepared horseradish and a hearty mustard.

504 calories	317 mg sodium
34.2 gr fat	10.8 gr saturated

Slow cooking is important as the boiling can toughen the beef.

Increase the cooking time for a larger brisket—allow about 1 hour per pound.

Cabbage may be prepared separately, but it is more flavorful when cooked in the beef water.

Other vegetables such as onions or carrots may be cooked in the pan with the cabbage.

Beef Gravy with Mushrooms

Serves 4

1 tablespoon olive oil
1 tablespoon butter
¼ pound mushrooms, sliced
2 tablespoons flour
1 cup beef stock, or stock or water
   combined with pan juice to make 1 cup

1. Heat **olive oil** and **butter** in a heavy skillet. Add **mushrooms** and sauté until lightly browned.

2. Sprinkle **mushrooms** with **flour** and toss to coat, cooking lightly for about 2 minutes.

3. Off heat, stir in the combined **stock** and **pan juice**. Return to heat and cook slowly, stirring to release particles clinging to the bottom and sides of the pan.

4. When gravy thickens, strain if desired and serve with any beef dish.

83 calories	225 mg sodium
6.9 gr fat	2.4 gr saturated

Use pan juices, seasoned to taste, to make gravy whenever possible as they will usually have the best flavor without containing an overabundance of salt.

Braised Beef

Braised Beef is not so much a specific dish as a style of cooking preferred for the less tender but flavorful cuts of meat. Meats or vegetables to be braised are first browned, then cooked (steamed, actually) in a tightly-closed pot. The long, slow cooking may be completed on top of the stove or in the oven.

Serves 4

3 ounces bacon (about 4 thin slices)
2 pounds beef (chuck or bottom round)
1 tablespoon flour
1 medium-sized onion, quartered
¼ teaspoon thyme
1 bay leaf
½ cup meat or vegetable broth

1. Cut **bacon** into ½-inch squares and fry lightly in a heavy, skillet or Dutch oven with a tight-fitting lid.

2. Cut **beef** to serving pieces about 1-inch square and brown well with the bacon.

3. Sprinkle **flour** over the meat and continue to cook, stirring to coat the meat and lightly brown the flour.

4. Add **onion** to the pan with **thyme** and **bay**. Pour **broth** over and bring to a boil.

5. Cover tightly and cook on top of the stove over low heat 1½ to 2½ hours; Check occasionally to be sure liquid has not cooked off; add more if necessary.

6. Remove meat and onion to a serving platter; keep warm. Boil down liquid in the pan to the desired consistency, stirring in any pieces clinging to the pan. Correct seasoning and serve 'as is' or strained.

526 calories	324 mg sodium
33.9 gr fat	13.0 gr saturated

Veal or pork or a combination of meats can be used in this recipe.

Carrots or celery, coarsely chopped, can be added with the onion.

Red wine can replace part or all of the broth in this recipe.

To prepare in the oven, bring liquid to a boil, cover tightly, and cook for about 2 hours at 350˚.

For a thicker gravy, blend 1 tablespoon of butter with 1 tablespoon of flour until smooth for each cup of liquid and whisk into the sauce or gravy, cooking until the liquid thickens.

To make this a one-dish meal, add other vegetables such as potatoes during the last 30 minutes of cooking.

Cooked vegetables, such as peas or green beans, can be added a few minutes before cooking is completed just to heat them through.

HEALTH NOTES:

For those concerned about saturated fats, about 3 grams per serving can be saved by substituting 2 tablespoons of olive oil for the bacon.

Sodium can be reduced by replacing the broth with water or a lightly seasoned meat or vegetable stock.

Shredded Beef

Braised in vinegar, this beef takes on a delightfully sharp flavor

Serves 4

---

2 tablespoons olive oil
¼ cup onion, finely chopped
2 pounds lean chuck, bottom round, or
   top round roast
¼ cup cider vinegar
1 bay leaf
2 garlic cloves, crushed
½ teaspoon salt

---

1. In a heavy pot, preferably a well-seasoned iron pot, heat **olive oil** and lightly sauté the **onion**.

2. Trim the fat completely from the **roast**. Place it in the pot and turn to brown the roast lightly on all sides.

3. Add the **vinegar, bay leaf, garlic,** and **salt** to the pot and bring to a boil. Lower the heat and simmer slowly, covered, on top of the stove or in a 300° oven for about 2 hours, or until meat is very tender.

4. When the roast is cooked, allow it to rest for about 10 minutes, then place it in a large bowl or roasting pan and shred the meat with two forks.

5. Strain the broth, if desired and correct **seasoning**. Mix broth with the shredded beef or set aside to make gravy.

---

541 calories	170 mg sodium
37.5 gr fat	12.8 gr saturated

Serve **Shredded Beef** with juices or gravy (see below) as part of a hot meal over rice, pasta, or mashed or baked potato; serve cold with a salad as a light luncheon or for a sandwich filling.

Shredded Beef makes a great barbecue— merely combine beef, with or without the broth, with a prepared barbecue sauce and heat through. Best if allowed to rest in the refrigerator for an hour or two.

To make gravy, use a fork to blend until smooth, 1 tablespoon of flour with 1 tablespoon of softened butter for each cup of liquid. Gradually stir butter 'pebbles' into the hot liquid and stir or whisk while cooking until the gravy thickens.

VARIATIONS:

Add chopped celery, green pepper, or carrots to the pot to cook with the meat and flavor the broth.

Mix a small amount of tomato paste into the vinegar before adding it to the pot..

Small onions or carrots can be cooked with the meat to accompany it as part of an entrée. Remove them from the pot with the meat before straining the liquid in the pot or making gravy.

Shredded Beef Sandwiches

Serves 4

Shredded Beef with juices
¾ cup onion, thinly sliced
½ cup green pepper, cut in thin strips
1 baguette about 24 inches long or 4 hard-crusted 6-inch rolls

1. Prepare *Shredded Beef* (previous recipe). Add the sliced **onion** and **green pepper** strips during the last half hour of cooking.

2. Divide **baguette** into 4 6-inch pieces and slice them three-quarters of the way through, leaving a 'hinge' at the back. Spread them open and fill with the **beef, onion, and pepper mixture** over each.

3. Sprinkle with strained **pan juice** or serve on the side for dipping.

817 calories	707 mg sodium
41.2 gr fat	13.6 gr saturated

VARIATIONS:

Mix in tomato sauce (vary the amount according to taste) with the pan liquid and boil briefly to thicken and blend. Strain and pour over sandwiches.

Top each open sandwich with a slice of provolone or Swiss cheese and melt under the broiler.

Horseradish Sauce

1 cup sour cream
¼ cup fresh or prepared horseradish, drained

1. Combine **sour cream** and **horseradish**.

2. Chill well before serving.

Minced parsley, chives, or onion may be added to this sauce that is an especially fine accompaniment to sandwiches, or to hot or cold fish or meats.

Beef Patties

Serves 4

1 pound ground beef
2 tablespoons onion, finely chopped
¼ cup soft bread crumbs
¼ teaspoon Worcestershire sauce
Salt & pepper
2 teaspoons olive oil

1. Lightly mix **ground beef** with **onion**, **bread crumbs**, and **Worcestershire sauce**; season with **salt** and **pepper** to taste. Shape into four patties.

2. Use a paper towel to spread a thin coating of the **olive oil** over the bottom of a heavy skillet. Heat the oil until very hot but not smoking. Brown the patties quickly on both sides, then lower the heat and cook until they are done to taste.

3. Serve on buns or with vegetables as part of an evening meal. As an entrée, patties may be served plain or accompanied by a sauce or gravy. (See recipe for *Beef Gravy with Mushrooms*).

314 calories	82 mg sodium
24.3 gr fat	9.2 gr saturated

The beef requires some fat to cook without drying out, about 20% fat content will do. Freshly ground beef is best, red but not so red as to show the use of artificial coloring.

Bread crumbs, although not absolutely necessary, help keep a patty moist and bind the meat when it is cooked in a skillet.

VARIATIONS:

Beef patties, like meat loaf, are easily enhanced with a variety of ingredients:

- In addition to onion, add chopped celery or green pepper.
- Instead of Worcestershire sauce, add soy sauce or a dash of hot sauce.
- Spice up beef patties with a bit of chili powder, curry powder, garlic, or jalapeño pepper finely chopped.

It's a pity that we've become so indoctrinated to tasteless fast food that we can no longer recall how good well-seasoned ground beef can be.

Without a doubt, the best way to cook a beef patty is on an open grill over a wood or charcoal fire. Our favorite second-best is to **cook with salt**:

Sprinkle a thin layer of salt over the bottom of an ungreased heavy iron skillet. When the skillet is very hot, add the beef patties; brown well on one side and turn to brown on the other. Reduce heat and continue cooking until done according to taste. If the pan is hot enough, the burger will not stick, the salt will not cling, and no fat need be used in the frying.

Reuben Burger

Serves 4

4 *Beef Patties*
8 slices rye bread
4 slices Swiss cheese
¼ cup Russian or Thousand Island
  dressing
½ cup sauerkraut, drained
4 tablespoons butter

1. Prepare and cook *Beef Patties* according to the recipe on the previous page.

2. Lightly toast the **rye bread** on one side and place a beef patty on the toasted side of 4 of the slices.

3. Top each patty with a slice of **Swiss cheese** and spread with Russian or Thousand Island **dressing**. Cover with a thin layer of **sauerkraut**, then a second bread slice, toasted side down.

4. **Butter** the outside of each sandwich and fry on a hot griddle or frying pan for about 3 minutes on each side or just long enough to brown the bread, melt the cheese a bit, and heat the sandwich through.

741 calories	1054 mg sodium
51.9 gr fat	23.3 gr saturated

Horseradish Sauce (see recipe) makes a great accompaniment for dipping.

Make your own concoction—Instead of a cheeseburger made by melting cheese on the burger as it cooks, then placing it on a cold bun, try the *Reuben Burger* technique, placing the cheese and condiments on slices of bread or rolls, then toasting them on a griddle or frying pan.

Seven Boy Curry

At one time, serving a curry dish provided a means to display one's wealth. Each accompaniment to the dish required a servant boy to present it; thus the number of condiments was an indication of the size of the host's staff.

Serves 4

2 tablespoons olive oil
¼ cup onion, finely chopped
2 pounds lean chuck, bottom round, or
   top round roast
2 tablespoons vinegar
Salt
4 tablespoons butter
1 cup celery, thinly sliced
4 tablespoons flour
1 tablespoon curry powder

1. Heat the **olive oil** in a heavy pot, preferably a seasoned iron kettle and sauté the **onion** lightly just until it is soft.

2. Add the **beef** to the pot and turn often to brown lightly on all sides. Add sufficient **boiling water** to cover the meat, then stir in the **vinegar** and a scant teaspoon of **salt**. Simmer, covered, for 2 hours, or until meat is very tender.

3. Remove meat and set aside. Boil the liquid in the pot down to make 2 cups. Set aside.

4. In the same kettle or a large saucepan, heat the **butter** and sauté the **celery** until it is barely soft. Sprinkle with **flour** and **curry powder**. Continue to cook, stirring to blend well, for 3 minutes.

5. Pour the **broth** into the kettle or pan and cook, stirring often, until thickened and smooth. Correct **seasoning**.

6. With two forks, shred the **beef** and add it to the sauce. Heat through and serve with condiments.

603 calories	256 mg sodium
40.1 gr fat	16.5 gr saturated

Curry Powder is a blend of a number of spices such as cardamom, chili, cinnamon, cloves, coriander, cumin, fennel, nutmeg, peppers, and turmeric, which provides the yellowish color. Authentic Indian curries vary markedly according to the region and the cook. Short of freshly grinding ones own, a lover of curry would do well to visit an Eastern or Oriental market to see what they have to offer.

Some traditional condiments for curry include:
• Grated coconut
• Raisins
• Grated orange rind
• Chopped peanuts
• Hard-cooked egg, finely chopped
• Candied ginger
• Chutney

Beef in Red Wine (Boeuf Bourguignonne)

Serves 4

2 tablespoons butter
½ pound fresh mushrooms, whole if
   small or quartered if large
3 slices bacon, diced
12 whole boiling or baby onions or 3
   medium onions quartered
2 pounds lean beef cut in 1½–inch cubes
2 tablespoons flour
1 cup dry red wine
1 cup beef broth
1 clove garlic, finely chopped
1 bay leaf
Salt & pepper

1. Heat the **butter** in a heavy skillet and sauté the **mushrooms** for 3 minutes, or just until they are soft. Remove mushrooms and set aside.

2. Add **bacon** to the skillet and cook just until fat has been rendered. Remove bacon with a slotted spoon and set aside with the mushrooms.

3. Sauté **onions** in the grease in the skillet, shaking or stirring to color them evenly. Set aside with mushrooms.

4. Use **bacon grease** from the skillet to lightly coat an oven dish.

5. Set aside all but a thin coating of the fat remaining the skillet. Brown **beef cubes** on all sides, taking care not to crowd them. Add more fat as needed. As cubes are browned, arrange in the oven dish.

6. Add fat to the skillet to make about 2 tablespoons. Stir in **flour** and cook for 2 minutes. Off the heat, pour in **wine** and **broth**, stirring until smooth. Add the **garlic** and **bay leaf**. Bring to a boil and pour over the beef. Cover tightly and bake at 300° for 2 hours.

7. Add reserved **mushrooms**, **bacon**, and **onions** to the dish and continue baking for 30 minutes or until beef is very tender.

8. Season to taste with **salt** and **pepper**. Serve garnished with parsley.

664 calories	459 mg sodium
38.0 gr fat	15.8 gr saturated

To complete the meal, potatoes can be added during the last 30 minutes.

Beef with Sour Cream(Beef Stroganoff)

2 tablespoons olive oil
½ cup onions, thinly sliced
1 pound lean beef, cut into strips
2 tablespoons butter
½ cup mushrooms, sliced
¼ cup beef stock, broth, or bouillon
Nutmeg
½ cup sour cream
Salt & pepper

1. Heat 1 tablespoon of the **olive oil** in a heavy skillet and sauté **onions** briefly, just until they take on a bit of color.

2. Add remaining **olive oil**, if needed. When it is hot but not smoking, add the **beef**; tossing to coat and brown the strips on all sides. Remove from pan and set aside.

3. Melt the **butter** in the same skillet and when it is very hot, sauté the **mushrooms** just until they are lightly browned.

4. Return **onions** and **beef** to the pan with the **broth** and a grating of **nutmeg**. Heat through, but do not boil.

5. Add **sour cream** and cook briefly to heat through and blend. Take care that the mixture does not boil after the sour cream is added. Correct the seasoning with **salt** and **pepper** and serve.

416 calories	207 mg sodium
33.5 gr fat	13.9 gr saturated

To prepare the beef: Cut into thin slices, then further thin and tenderize the slices by placing them between two sheets of wax paper or clear food wrap and pounding gently with a food mallet, working from the center of the slices toward the outer edges. If a food mallet is not available, use a heavy spoon or a smooth-bottomed cup or bowl.
Beef should then be cut into thin strips so as to minimize cooking time.

When sour cream is exposed to excessive heat, it separates or curdles. We know of no way to recover from the condition except perhaps to strain the sauce and whisk in a bit of fresh, cold sour cream. The sauce is still edible, it has merely lost its fine texture.

VARIATIONS:

Tomato paste is a common addition in recipes for Stroganoff. If desired, combine a teaspoonful with the beef broth before adding the broth to the pan.

Make _Chicken Stroganoff_ with boneless chicken breasts cut into thin strips or prepare it from leftover chicken.

Cooked peas can be added at the same time as the sour cream. It may not be classic Stroganoff, but it is delicious.

Family Meat Loaf

Serves 4

1 tablespoon olive oil
2 tablespoons onion, finely chopped
1 pound ground beef
1 egg, beaten
1 cup soft bread crumbs
1 teaspoon salt
¼ teaspoon pepper
¼ cup beef broth

1. Heat **olive oil** in a heavy skillet and sauté the **onion** until lightly browned.

2. Lightly, but thoroughly, combine **onion** with **ground beef**, beaten **egg**, **bread crumbs**, **salt**, and **pepper**.

3. Form meat mixture into a loaf and place it in a lightly greased baking pan. Bake for 40 minutes in a 350° oven, basting after about 15 minutes with the broth and occasionally thereafter with pan juices.

4. Remove loaf from the oven and allow to rest for at least 10 minutes before slicing.

367 calories	275 mg sodium
27.2 gr fat	9.9 gr saturated

Mix meat loaf ingredients thoroughly but with care in order to produce a lightly textured loaf. The two favored methods are to use the hands, taking care not to pack the ingredients tightly, or to combine the ingredients in a large bowl with the aid of two forks.

VARIATIONS:

Meat loaf generally means *ground beef loaf*; however, most meat loaf recipes can be made up partly of pork or veal according to the cook's preference.

Variations for meat loaf are endless, such as the use of cornbread or cracker crumbs instead of bread crumbs, the inclusion of milk or cream, adding spinach, potato, or rice. Recipes for some distinct variations such as *Tex-Mex Loaf*, *Italian Loaf*, and *Spinach Loaf* are on the following pages.

To this basic recipe may be added:
Finely chopped celery or green pepper that has been lightly sautéed
Chopped fresh or canned tomato, well-drained
Chopped parsley, basil, or chives
Prepared horseradish or finely chopped garlic
Dry or prepared mustard
Worcestershire sauce or soy sauce

Add a topping of catsup or tomato sauce for the last 10 minutes of cooking.

Beef-Spinach Loaf

1 tablespoon olive oil
3 tablespoons onion, finely chopped
8 ounces fresh spinach
1 pound ground beef
¼ teaspoon nutmeg, freshly grated
1 egg, lightly beaten
½ cup soft bread crumbs
1 teaspoon salt
¼ teaspoon pepper
¼ cup vegetable or chicken broth

1. Heat **olive oil** in a large heavy skillet and sauté the **onion** until just softened.

2. Rinse **spinach** in several changes of water until no grit settles in the bottom of the container. Shake off excess water; do not pat dry. Place in the skillet and cover lightly. Cook for 3 minutes or until the leaves are wilted, tossing to heat evenly.

3. Using the hands or two forks, lightly combine the **onion**, **beef**, **spinach**, **nutmeg**, **egg**, **bread crumbs**, **salt**, and **pepper**.

4. Form into a loaf and place in a lightly greased baking pan. Bake for 40 minutes in a 350° oven, basting occasionally, first with the broth, then with pan juices.

5. Remove loaf from the oven and allow to rest for at least 10 minutes before slicing.

366 calories	377 mg sodium
27.0 gr fat	9.9 gr saturated

To substitute frozen spinach for the fresh, merely defrost it.

VARIATIONS:

A bit of minced garlic is a pleasant addition to this loaf. Add it to the skillet with spinach, taking care that it doesn't scorch.

Bake loaf in a ring mold and serve with mashed potatoes, peas, winter squash, small whole carrots or some other vegetable in the center for an attractive presentation.

Italian Meat Loaf

Serves 4

1 tablespoon olive oil
2 tablespoons onion, finely chopped
1 pound ground meat made up of equal
  parts beef, pork, & veal
1 egg, beaten
1 cup soft bread crumbs
½ teaspoon oregano
½ teaspoon basil
1 teaspoon parsley
1 clove garlic, minced
1 tablespoon Parmesan cheese, grated
1 teaspoon salt
¼ teaspoon pepper
¼ cup beef broth

1. Heat **olive oil** in a small skillet and sauté the **onion** until lightly browned.

2. Using the hands or two forks, lightly combine the **onion** with the **ground meat, egg, bread crumbs, oregano, basil, parsley, garlic, Parmesan cheese, salt,** and **pepper.**

3. Form into a loaf and place in a lightly greased baking pan. Bake for about 40 minutes in a 350° oven. Baste occasionally with the broth.

4. Remove from the oven and allow to rest for at least 10 minutes before slicing.

326 calories	397 mg sodium
21.8 gr fat	7.5 gr saturated

COOK'S NOTES:

A combination of meats, already ground and packaged together, may be found in the grocer's refrigerator case. Our favorite is the offer of packaged meats that the butcher will grind for you when you buy it.

The ratio of meats may be varied, but take care not to include too much veal which will dry the loaf. If sausage is added, keep it modest as it may add too much fat.

For an elegant presentation, form the loaf into a roll about 3 inches in diameter. (Adjust cooking time for a small loaf if necessary to avoid overcooking.) To serve, ladle tomato sauce (see recipe next page) onto individual plates and arrange sliced rounds of the meat over the sauce. Garnish with parsley.

Small rounds of sliced meat loaf can be arranged over servings of pasta.

VARIATIONS:

Add fresh or canned tomatoes that have been well-drained and finely chopped.

Add pitted green or black olives to the meat mixture.

Anchovies, mashed or finely chopped, can be added to the meat mixture for flavoring, or use whole anchovies to garnish each serving.

Tomato Sauce for Meat Loaf

2 cups Italian tomatoes, canned
1 clove garlic, crushed
1 to 2 teaspoons fresh basil, chopped or
½ teaspoon dried basil, crushed
1 teaspoon fresh oregano, chopped or ¼
teaspoon dried oregano, crushed
Pinch of sugar
Salt & pepper

1. Cook **tomatoes with canning liquid** over high heat until the mixture thickens slightly, stirring frequently to keep sauce from burning on the bottom.

2. Off the heat, add the **garlic, basil, oregano,** and **sugar** with **salt** and **pepper** to taste. Stir to combine with the warm sauce. Cover and allow to stand for a few minutes to blend the flavors.

3. Discard the crushed garlic clove before serving.

Use a bit of this sauce to moisten meat loaf ingredients, use it to baste a meat loaf, or serve it heated on the side.

Just a reminder that leftover meat loaf makes great sandwiches.

Tex-Mex Meat Loaf

Serves 4

1 tablespoon olive oil
2 tablespoons onion, chopped
2 tablespoons green pepper, chopped
1 egg, lightly beaten
¼ cup milk
1 pound ground beef
1 cup cracker crumbs
2 tablespoons jalapeño peppers, chopped
1 teaspoon salt
¼ teaspoon pepper

1. Heat **olive oil** and lightly sauté the **onion** and **green pepper**.

2. Combine **egg** and **milk**.

3. With hands or two forks, lightly combine the sautéed **onion** and **pepper** with the **egg mixture**, **ground beef**, **cracker crumbs**, **jalapeños**, **salt**, and **pepper**.

4. Form mixture into a loaf and place in a lightly greased baking pan. Bake for about 40 minutes in a 350° oven.

5. If loaf becomes dry, baste with a bit of broth, or add a little water to the bottom of the pan and cover with foil.

6. Allow cooked loaf to rest for 10 minutes. Serve meat sliced with *Picante Sauce* on the side.

446 calories	265 mg sodium
27.1 gr fat	9.8 gr saturated

Picante Sauce

1 tablespoon olive oil
¼ cup onion, finely chopped
¼ cup green pepper, finely chopped
2 cloves garlic, minced
½ teaspoon chili powder
1 tablespoon vinegar
1 cup canned tomato pieces
Salt & pepper to taste

1. Heat olive oil in a small saucepan and lightly sauté onion and green pepper.

2. Add remaining ingredients, bring to a boil, and allow to simmer for about 20 minutes or until slightly thickened.

3. This sauce is best if allowed to rest for a few hours or overnight.

COOK'S NOTES:

Adjust the amount of garlic, chili powder, and vinegar to suit personal taste.

Picante Sauce **is suitable for** serving hot or cold with meat, poultry, or fish.

The heat from jalapeño peppers can vary greatly based on age, where the peppers were grown, etc. Adjust the quantity in recipes depending on their strength and your personal taste.

For variety, other hot peppers may be substituted for jalapeños.

Brandied Beef

Serves 6

3 tablespoons butter
3 pounds lean stew beef, cubed
Thin strips of zest from 1 orange
2 cups onions, thinly sliced
½ cup beef broth
½ cup brandy
2 cloves garlic, crushed
2 cups carrots, cut into julienne strips
2 tablespoons parsley, chopped
1 tablespoon lemon rind, grated
Salt

1. Heat **butter** in a heavy covered kettle until foaming. Brown **beef** well on all sides, in batches so as not to crowd the meat.

2. Return beef to the pan with **orange zest, onions, broth,** ¼ cup of the **brandy,** and **garlic.** Cook, covered, over low heat for 2 hours or until beef is fork-tender

3. When beef is done, discard **garlic.** Add **carrots** to the pan and cook for 30 minutes.

4. With a slotted spoon, transfer meat and vegetables to a serving platter and keep warm.

5. Add **parsley, lemon rind,** and remaining **brandy** to the pan. Season with **salt** to taste. Cook the sauce briefly and serve over the meat and vegetables.

541 calories	256 mg sodium
27.4 gr fat	12.0 gr saturated

COOK'S NOTE: For *zest,* peel the orange with a vegetable peeler or (if you have a steady hand) with a very sharp knife. Use only the thin outer skin, eliminating the bitter white underneath, and cut into fine julienne strips.

Carbonnade Flamande

Serves 8

5 tablespoons each, butter and olive oil
4 pound top round, sliced thin
4 cups onions, thinly sliced
¼ teaspoon sugar
1½ cups stout or ale, flat
1½ teaspoons rosemary
1 clove garlic, minced
2 tablespoons wine vinegar
1 tablespoon Dijon-style mustard

1. Heat butter and oil in a large lidded skillet and brown the beef. Sauté in batches and toss to brown evenly. Set aside.

2. Add onions to the fat and juices left in the pan and cook slowly until almost caramelized, stirring in sugar as the onions begin to brown.

3. Return beef to the pan with stout, rosemary, and garlic. Simmer, covered, until the beef is tender. Season with salt and pepper to taste.

4. Stir in vinegar and mustard. Cook for a few minutes to blend flavors.

579 calories	213 mg sodium
37.3 gr fat	14.0 gr saturated

Beef & Peppers

Serves 4

1 pound round steak, about ½ inch thick
½ cup beef broth
¼ cup soy sauce
½ teaspoon ginger root, minced
½ teaspoon sugar
1 clove garlic, minced
2 green peppers
1 medium onion
2 tablespoons olive oil
2 tablespoons cornstarch
1 cup cherry tomatoes, halved

1. Cut **steak** into thin strips across the grain.
2. Combine **broth, soy sauce, ginger, sugar,** and **garlic**. Add **steak**; marinate 1 hour.
3. Quarter **peppers**; remove seeds and membranes. Cut into ¼-inch slices.
4. Trim **onion** and cut lengthwise into ½-inch slices.
5. Heat **oil** in a skillet or wok. Sauté **peppers** and **onion** just until they are soft. Remove with a slotted spoon and set aside.
6. Remove **steak** from the marinade and reserve the liquid. Pat the meat dry and sauté in the same pan, turning until well-browned. Add more oil if needed.
7. Pour reserved **marinade** and ½ cup **hot water** into the pan with the meat. Cover and simmer until meat is almost tender, about 30 minutes.

8. Blend **cornstarch** into ¼ cup water until smooth. Add to the pan with the reserved **peppers** and **onions** and **tomatoes**. Simmer while stirring until the liquid thickens. Serve over rice.

383 calories	992 mg sodium
22.0 gr fat	6.7 gr saturated

Sweet & Sour Roast

Serves 6

1 tablespoon butter
1 tablespoon olive oil
¼ cup onion, thinly sliced
¼ cup carrot, thinly sliced
3-pound lean beef roast
1½ cups beer, flat
1 tablespoon vinegar
1 teaspoon sugar
½ teaspoon dried thyme
1 bay leaf
Salt & pepper

1. Heat **butter** and **oil** in a heavy kettle until very hot but not smoking. Sauté the **onion** and **carrot**, stirring to brown evenly and well without scorching.

2. Place **roast** in the kettle and brown on all sides to seal the meat. Add **beer**, **vinegar**, **sugar**, **thyme**, **bay leaf**, and 1 teaspoon of **black pepper**.

3. Bring the liquid to a boil, then reduce heat and simmer slowly for 1 to 2 hours or until meat is fork-tender. Remove roast and rest for 10 minutes before slicing.

4. Season juices with **salt** and **pepper** to taste. Strain and serve over sliced or shredded beef.

468 calories	137 mg sodium
25.6 gr fat	9.9 gr saturated

Calf's Liver with Onion

Serves 4

1 cup onion, thinly sliced
¼ cup dry white wine
½ teaspoon curry powder
2 tablespoons butter, melted
1½ pounds calf's liver, sliced
1 tart apple, cored and sliced

1. In a small saucepan, simmer the **onion** in the **wine** for 10 minutes or until most of the liquid is absorbed. Stir in **curry powder** and 1 tablespoon of the **butter**.

2. Remove the thin outer skin and veins from the **liver**. Rinse and pat dry. Brush lightly with the remaining **butter**.

3. Place **liver slices** in a shallow pan and broil about 4 inches from the heat for 3 minutes.

4. Remove liver from the oven and turn. Surround with the **onions** and **apple** slices. Return to the oven and broil for 3 minutes on the second side.

313 calories	165 mg sodium
13.3 gr fat	6.3 gr saturated

Take care not to overcook liver—it is most tender when cooked through, that is, no longer bloody, but with a bit of pink remaining in the center.

Stuffed Liver

Serves 4

4 slices calf's liver, about 1½ pounds total
2 tablespoons flour
2 tablespoons butter
½ cup onion, thinly sliced
¼ cup mushrooms, minced
¾ cup soft bread crumbs
Salt & pepper
4 slices bacon, halved
1 cup dry white wine

1. Remove thin outer skin and veins from the **liver**. Rinse and pat dry. Dust lightly with **flour**.

2. Heat the **butter** in a heavy skillet and sauté the **liver** for 2 minutes on each side. Arrange in a single layer in a lightly greased oven dish.

3. Sauté **onions** in the same skillet until they are soft. Add the **mushrooms** and lower the heat, cooking just until mushrooms give off some moisture.

4. Off the heat, combine the onion-mushroom mixture with the **bread crumbs**. Season with **salt** and **pepper** to taste.

5. Divide the stuffing among the **liver slices** and spread to form an even layer. Top with **bacon** slices and pour **wine** into the dish.

6. Bake at 325° for 30 minutes or just until liver is tender.

| 399 calories | 311 mg sodium |
| 16.8 gr fat | 7.5 gr saturated |

Beef, chicken, or vegetable broth or water can replace the wine.

Veal Cordon Bleu

Serves 4

8 veal cutlets, about 1½ pounds total
2 tablespoons olive oil
¼ pound smoked ham or prosciutto,
  sliced thin
¼ pound Swiss cheese, sliced thin
½ cup flour
1 egg, lightly beaten with 1
  tablespoon water
½ cup bread or cracker crumbs, sifted

1. Lightly pound **cutlets** to ¼-inch thickness.

2. Heat **oil** in a heavy skillet and brown the veal quickly—about 2 minutes per side Meat should be barely cooked through.

3. Place a thin slice of **ham** and **cheese** on four of the cutlets, then top with the remaining four cutlets.

4. Line up the **flour**, **egg mixture**, and **crumbs** in individual containers such as plates or pie tins.

5. Dip stuffed **cutlets**, one at a time, into **flour**; shake to remove any excess, then dip in the **egg mixture**, and finally in the **crumbs**. As each is coated, place in an oven dish in a single layer.

6. Bake in a 350° oven for about 10 minutes, then turn the cutlets and bake for 5 minutes longer or until top is crisp.

614 calories	5967 mg sodium
35.5 gr fat	17.6 gr saturated

Veal in Sherry Sauce

Serves 4

1½ pounds ground veal
1 cup heavy cream
4 egg yolks, lightly beaten
Salt & pepper
2 tablespoons olive oil
½ pound fresh mushrooms, sliced
Pinch of sage
2 tablespoons cream sherry

1. With two forks, gently combine the **veal**, ¼ cup of the **cream**, and the **egg yolks**. Season with **salt** and **pepper** to taste. Shape into 4 patties.

2. Heat **olive oil** in a heavy skillet until very hot but not smoking and brown the patties for about 3 minutes on each side. Set aside and keep warm.

3. Add **mushrooms** to the pan and sauté them until they are lightly colored.

4. Pour the remaining **cream** into the skillet and simmer for 3 minutes, stirring in the pan juices. Add the **sherry** and continue to cook, stirring, for 2 minutes.

5. Serve sauce over the patties accompanied by rice or pasta.

609 calories	171 mg sodium
46.0 gr fat	21.0 gr saturated

Veal with Artichokes

Serves 4

4 veal cutlets, ¼ inch thick, about 1½
   pounds total
1 tablespoon olive oil
1 tablespoon butter
4 canned artichoke hearts, drained
4 mushroom caps
½ cup light cream
½ cup beef broth
Salt & pepper

1. Place **cutlets** between two sheets of waxed paper or clear food wrap and pound lightly, working from the center to the edges, to tenderize them.

2. Heat **olive oil** and **butter** in a heavy skillet until very hot but not smoking. Sauté **veal** 3 minutes on a side. Arrange in a lightly buttered baking dish in a single layer.

3. Top each cutlet with an **artichoke heart** and a **mushroom cap**.

4. Whisk **cream** into the drippings in the skillet, then add **beef broth**. Bring to a boil and season with **salt** and **pepper** to taste. Pour into the oven dish.

5. Bake at 450° for 15 minutes, or until the meat is tender.

6. Remove the cutlets with their toppings to a serving dish and serve with the sauce.

401 calories	317 mg sodium
25.7 gr fat	11.7 gr saturated

Fresh artichoke hearts should be steamed until just soft. Cook frozen artichokes according to package directions.

The cutlets can also be topped with slices of green or red pepper that have been lightly sautéed, or with sliced black olives.

Breaded Veal Cutlet (Wiener Schnitzel)

1½ pounds veal cutlet
2 tablespoons prepared mustard
½ teaspoon Worcestershire sauce
½ cup flour
1 egg, lightly beaten with 1
  tablespoon water
½ cup bread or cracker crumbs, sifted
½ cup butter

1. If **cutlets** are very large, cut to about 3-inch squares. Place cutlets, one at a time, between two sheets of wax paper or clear film wrap. On a flat surface, gently pound the meat with a kitchen mallet or the dull side of a cleaver, working from the center to the edges. Turn and pound on the other side until cutlets are about ¼-inch thick.

2. Mix **mustard** and **Worcestershire sauce** in a small container. Brush both sides of meat with a thin coating of the mixture. Set aside.

3. Line up the **flour**, **egg mixture**, and **crumbs** in individual containers such as plates or pie tins.

4. Melt **butter** in a heavy skillet.

5. Dip **cutlets**, one at a time, into the **flour**; shake to remove any excess, then dip in the **egg mixture**, and finally in the **crumbs**. As each is coated, place in the skillet over low heat and brown for about 2 minutes on each side. Turn once more to cook through, 5 to 7 minutes.

582 calories	583 mg sodium
36.9 gr fat	19.6 gr saturated

An even coating of bread or cracker crumbs is necessary to cook evenly. Some cooks recommend resting the cutlets on a rack for a couple of minutes after brushing with the mustard mixture.

Take care not to crowd the meat in the skillet or it will steam rather than sauté. Cook in two or three batches if necessary.

VARIATIONS:

This classic Viennese recipe is reputed to have actually originated in France. As with most traditional dishes, there are as many variations as there are cooks. Some claim that for the dish to be authentic, the cutlets must be deep-fried rather than pan fried. Others call for only enough fat or oil to coat the bottom of a skillet (see **Health Notes**).

The mustard mixture is totally eliminated by some—the cutlets are simply dried, seasoned with salt and pepper, and coated with crumbs before sautéing.

The meat may be served topped with anchovies and capers, or with rings of fried onion.

HEALTH NOTES:

Substituting ¼ cup olive oil for half the butter will add 20 calories and 2 grams of total fat, but reduces saturated fat by 5.5 grams and sodium by 230 mg. per serving, a significant improvement.

Both calories and fat can be reduced by using only as much olive oil or butter, or combination of the two, necessary to lightly coat the pan.

Veal with Lemon
(Veal Piccata)

Serves 4

1½ pounds veal cutlets, about ¼ inch
  thick
Flour
Salt & pepper
2 tablespoons butter
2 tablespoons olive oil
¼ cup dry white wine
3 tablespoons fresh lemon juice
Thin lemon slices
Chopped parsley

1. If **cutlets** are very large, cut to about 3 inches square. Place between sheets of waxed paper or clear food wrap and pound lightly to flatten.

2. Dust the meat with a mixture of **flour**, **salt**, and **pepper**.

3. Heat enough of the **butter** and **olive oil** to coat the bottom of a heavy skillet until very hot but not smoking. Sauté **cutlets** in single layers, adding more oil and butter as needed. Cooking time should be brief, about 2 minutes per side.

4. Remove meat, pour off fat, and add **wine** to the pan. Stir in any brown bits that cling to the skillet. When the wine begins to boil, mix in the **lemon juice** and return the meat to the pan. Stir and turn the meat to coat with the sauce.

5. Place the meat on a serving platter. Strain any remaining sauce, pour over the meat, and garnish with thin **lemon slices** and chopped **parsley**. Serve with rice or pasta in a light sauce.

376 calories	199 mg sodium
24.3 gr fat	9.2 gr saturated

Veal Parmigiana

Serves 4

4 tablespoons olive oil
¼ cup onion, finely chopped
1½ cups canned tomatoes, diced, with juice
½ teaspoon basil
½ teaspoon oregano
Salt & pepper
1½ pounds veal cutlet, thinly sliced
1 egg, lightly beaten
¼ cup Parmesan cheese, grated
¼ cup fine bread crumbs
½ cup mozzarella cheese, shredded

1. Heat 2 tablespoons of the **olive oil** in a heavy skillet or saucepan. Sauté **onion** until lightly colored.

2. Add **tomatoes with canning juice, basil,** and the **oregano.** Simmer for 20 minutes or until the sauce has cooked down and thickened somewhat. Season with **salt** and **pepper** to taste.

3. While sauce cooks, prepare the meat: Place **cutlets** between sheets of wax paper or clear food wrap and pound them gently, working from the center to the edges, to tenderize and thin them a bit.

4. Beat the **egg** with 2 teaspoons of **water** and set aside in a shallow pan or bowl.

5. Combine **Parmesan cheese** and **bread crumbs**; set aside on a plate.

6. Heat the remaining **olive oil** in a heavy skillet until it is very hot but not smoking.

7. Dip **cutlets** in the **egg mixture,** draining off any excess, then in the **cheese mixture,** and sauté quickly, about 2 minutes on each side.

8. Cover the bottom of an oven dish with a thin layer of the **tomato sauce.** Arrange **cutlets** over the sauce in a single layer. Sprinkle with shredded **mozzarella** and cover with the remaining **sauce.**

9. Bake at 350° for 30 minutes, or until the mixture is heated through.

540 calories	544 mg sodium
35.8 gr fat	12.6 gr saturated

Double the recipe for tomato sauce and combine half with a bowl of pasta to serve with the *Veal Parmigiana*.

Zesty Pork Chops

Serves 4

2 tablespoons olive oil
¼ cup onion, thinly sliced
¼ cup green pepper, thinly sliced
1 tablespoon commercial brown
   seasoning sauce or teriyaki sauce
4 thick pork chops, about 2 pounds total
½ cup chicken broth
¼ cup dry white wine
Salt & pepper

1. Heat **olive oil** in a heavy skillet and sauté **onion** and **green pepper** just until soft. Set aside.

2. Combine the **brown sauce** with ¼ cup of **water** and brush liberally over the **pork chops.**

3. Brown the **chops** on both sides in **oil** remaining in the skillet. Return **onion** and **pepper** to the pan. Pour in the **broth** and **wine.**

4. Simmer, tightly covered, for 40 minutes or until the pork is tender.

5. Remove the pork to a serving platter and top with the onions and peppers.

6. Skim excess fat from the pan and season the liquid to taste with **salt** and **pepper.** Serve over the chops.

468 calories	362 mg sodium
35.2 gr fat	10.8 gr saturated

Pork with Mustard Sauce

Serves 4

4 thick pork chops, about 2 pounds total
2 tablespoons olive oil
¼ cup white wine
2 tablespoons flour
¼ cup prepared mustard
1 cup light cream
½ teaspoon lemon rind, grated
Salt & pepper

1. Trim **chops** of excess fat, leaving not more than ¼ inch around the edges.

2. Heat **olive oil** in a heavy skillet large enough to contain the chops in one layer. Brown the chops on both sides. Pour **wine** into the pan and simmer lightly, covered, for 40 minutes or until the chops are cooked through and tender. Set aside and keep warm.

3. Skim excess fat from the pan juices, leaving about 2 tablespoons. Stir the **flour** into the liquids remaining in the pan and cook for 2 minutes. Stir in the **mustard,** then the **cream,** and bring to a boil. Remove from the heat and add the **lemon rind.** Season with **salt** and **pepper** to taste.

4. Serve mustard sauce over the pork chops.

619 calories	126 mg sodium
50.1 gr fat	20.1 gr saturated